Forest H. Belt's

Easi-Guide

to

INDOOR HOME REPAIRS

By

John and Melba Statzer

Photography by

Treva J. Moon and Forest H. Belt

 HOWARD W. SAMS & CO., INC.
THE BOBBS-MERRILL CO., INC.
INDIANAPOLIS · KANSAS CITY · NEW YORK

Introduction

"They just don't build stuff like they used to." That's a common cry nowadays, and it's true in many respects. The pride of craftsmanship seems to have been subjugated to the economics of production. Whatever you buy, you can almost depend on its needing some kind of repairs and servicing before very long. This truism is the bane of almost any homeowner's existence. There always seems to be something needing repair.

But that's only one facet of the problem. The next question, once you know things need fixing, is: who can you get to fix them? The answer, in too many cases, is no one—at least not easily, not promptly, and not economically. Despite the dire need, the field of servicing and repairs has fallen out of favor with young men who could learn the skills to maintain equipment in modern homes, You may have to do it yourself . . . hence this book.

If you think it's easy to find a general repair expert, just pick up the telephone book and try. If you find one, phone and ask how long before he could take care of a repair for you.

Even specialists seem in such short supply that it takes a week or more to get help. Call a plumber or electrician, plastering expert, or appliance technician. You'll find most of them with a nearly impossible backlog of work.

The home-repair expert who co-authors this book, John B. Statzer, has spent most of his working life dealing with home systems—keeping them running smoothly and preventing the houses from falling down around their owners' ears. Recently retired, he has been one of a now-vanishing breed, the professional home-repair technician. In the community where John Statzer has lived and worked, he's known as a top-grade all-around fix-it man. Just ask any of his past customers. From foundation to roof, whatever might go wrong in a house, he could be depended on to fix it—and fix it right. If something needed to be added, he could do it. Overhauled, sure. Cleaned and adjusted, you bet.

You should have heard the furor when he announced his intention to retire and move away. "What on earth will we do?" "Can't you do this (or that) little job before you go?" All the "wait awhile" repairs within a 20-mile radius suddenly became top priority. He could have worked six more months on one month's calls. But he did retire, and the homeowners in that locality now face the same difficulty that others do all over the country. There simply are no general repair experts around.

John Statzer is not a writer. Putting together a book like this to help old customers—and thousands more homeowners—just didn't seem to him like something he could do. But Melba Statzer, his wife, found the idea suited her fine. So the co-authorship was formed. John Statzer would work with the photographer (Treva Moon, who happens to be their daughter) and then explain the procedures to Melba Statzer, who in turn would write them to suit the photographs and the format of this book.

You are about to read the result, another in my series of Forest H. Belt's Easi-Guides. The authors and I hope this book at least partly takes the place of a professional home-repair expert. You can be your own fixer. Hundreds of little repairs, you can do yourself. In light of the scarcity of experts and the high cost when you do find one, taking care of your own maintenance and repairs may be the only practical way. You'll find this book full of work- and money-saving aids to keeping your house intact and running.

FOREST H. BELT

Contents

Chapter 1

In the Interest of Home Safety

Accidents happen at home more than anywhere else. Many of them occur while some kind of repairs are being attempted. These and other home accidents can be prevented if you'll observe a few simple precautions. There are right and wrong ways to do things. Usually, the safest method is the most efficient anyway. But even when it's slower, the safe way is the only right way. This first chapter introduces some of the dangers you may encounter in making your own home repairs and shows how you can avoid injury and inconvenience.

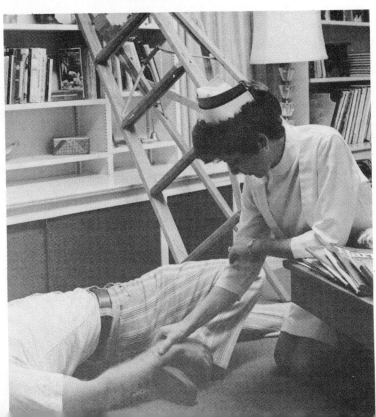

Reaching to high places constitutes a major hazard. Rule one is that you should never ask a chair to do the work of a ladder. But even with a ladder, misuse such as shown here is just begging for trouble.

NEVER stand on top of a ladder. With nothing to brace yourself against, you run a high risk of losing your balance. One slip means an almost certain fall. If you happen to lean against the wall, the leverage of your high position can too easily push the ladder over.

Beware of metal ladders whenever you're doing electrical repairs. They could set up conditions for a shock. Dry wood is more of an electrical insulator, while aluminum is a very good conductor. Even carrying a metal ladder, you can accidentally strike and break a hanging light bulb and receive a severe shock— particularly in a basement or a house on a concrete slab.

Most metal stepladders are not as sturdy as wooden ones. They have a tendency to twist or sway under the stress of your weight. This could cause you to lose balance and fall, or let the ladder tip over. Further, the swaying might cause you to miss a nail you're driving, slip off a screw head, or otherwise trigger a different accident.

The right way. Okay, first of all, open the ladder to its full extension. If there's a bucket shelf, open that out, as it helps brace the ladder.

Test for wobbling. If the ladder shakes easily, some of the screws may need tightening. If it still seems unsteady, it might be necessary to add a couple of cross-strip braces. Fasten them on with screws, not nails (which would just work loose in a short time).

And then stand at least two rungs below the top, even on shorter ladders. That gives you some leverage and bracing to maintain your balance.

Electrical repairs offer your next greatest hazard. Know where to find the main switch or master disconnect. Usually, it's at the top of the electrical service box. It often is marked MAIN. In case of an electrical emergency, such as a cord sputtering sparks, or if you smell insulation burning, pull the master switch. That cuts off all electricity to your house wiring while you hunt or repair the source of trouble.

Sometimes this disconnect is not a switch but a large black block containing big, heavy cartridge fuses (which you can't see from the outside). There may be two of these blocks, just as there are two main switches pictured above. Grasp the handles of the fuse blocks and pull hard, till they come out. That removes all power while you do your repair work.

Never work on any appliance, lamp, or electrical outlet until the power to it is disconnected. Turn off the circuits for the area you plan to work in, by removing fuses or opening up (turning off) the switch-type breakers. If you have any doubts in your mind about which fuse or breaker opens the circuit, pull the main switch.

As a further precaution, always unplug any electrical tool before replacing bits or blades. The danger may be in its inadvertently turning on, more than any electrical worry.

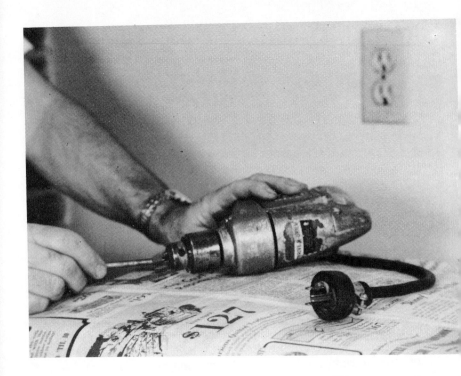

Avoid using metal receptacle plates. Careless wiring could come into contact with one, offering a shock hazard unless plate, box, and conduit are properly grounded. A faulty outlet with metal plate could cause an appliance you plug in there to shock you. If you move into a house that has this type of receptacle cover, especially in the kitchen or bathroom, disconnect the main power and change them to plastic.

Also have the electrical gounding of all conduits or armored-type cables checked by a licensed electrician, whenever you move into a house that's new to you. If you don't, you may work yourself into a hidden booby trap sometime when you're attempting minor repairs.

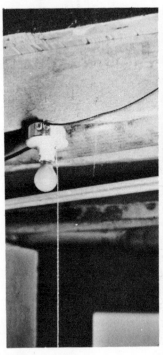

Some homes are full of electrical hazards. A dangerous combination in many basements is depicted here. The light has a metal pull chain. It hangs above a floor that is often wet. Water is a good conductor of electricity and makes concrete a better-than-usual conductor. If you're standing on this wet floor and take hold of the metal pull chain to turn the light on or off, you could complete an electrical circuit with your body. The shock can be serious, if not fatal.

The one in these pictures actually was dangerous, owing to a poorly taped connection inside the box and to the use of nonarmored wiring. It had been that way two years, but was discovered when a string pull broke and was replaced by a metal one. The shock wasn't fatal but it could have been. Have the grounds checked and use only STRING pulls. Keep them dry (no wet hands).

Here's another potential hazard: wet hands, with a kitchen appliance nearby. KEEP appliances AWAY from sinks and grounded metal cabinets, screens, pipes, etc. The safest practice is to use three-wire grounded plugs. If a short circuit occurs in the appliance, which might otherwise make the case dangerous to touch, the third wire carries the "short" to ground. The fault causes nothing more serious than a blown fuse or a circuit breaker kicked open. And that's the purpose of fuses and breakers.

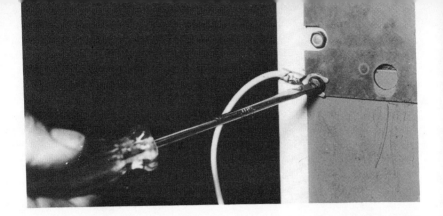

Here's another minor "repair" you can make to assure electrical safety. Appliances such as washers and dryers should always be grounded to a cold-water line. This is not because they're normally dangerous. It's because they're dangerous IF a short or electrical leakage develops in them. A good ground protects the user from shock in those cases.

Take a piece of AWG-14 or larger wire long enough to reach from the appliance to the nearest cold-water pipe (never hot-water). Scrape the wire for about a half-inch at both ends. Attach a spade lug at one end of the wire. That's a little U-shape terminal; most hardware or electrical stores have them. Push the wire end into the lug hole and crimp the tabs tight with a pair of pliers. Solder the wire to the lug if you know how.

Next, loosen one of the screws that fasten the back panel of the appliance. Scrape off paint around the screw-hole, for both back cover and appliance cabinet. Slide the fork of the lug around the screw, under the head, and tighten the screw (clockwise).

Attach a grounding pipe clamp tightly to the cold-water pipe. Loosen the wire-hole screw on the clamp. Slide the free end of the grounding wire from the appliance into the clamp behind the screw. Tighten.

Watch out for bent or broken appliance plugs and for insulation worn off the cord near the plug. These are a potential source of short circuit, shock, and even fire. Plugs and cords wear down from age or from being roughly handled. For example, yanking a plug out of a receptacle by the cord instead of taking hold of the plug itself is lazy and contributes heavily to wear and tear—and, eventually, danger.

The best repair is a whole new cord, complete with plug molded on. Or, you can just put a new plug on, if the rest of the cord is not worn. Page 95 shows how, in detail.

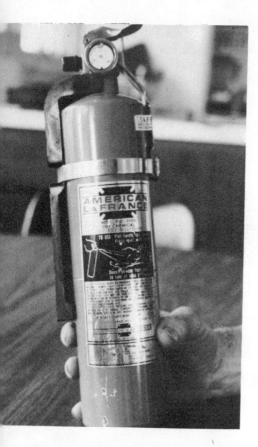

Speaking of fire hazards, no home should be without a good fire extinguisher. Too many people rely on the cheap pressure-can type. These have a relatively short life. Ever reach for a can of hair spray or shaving cream only to find that, although the pressurized can obviously has something in it, nothing comes out? The same thing can happen with such fire extinguishers.

Better extinguishers cost more, but they last longer, and are refillable. A gauge on top indicates the amount of pressure inside, which is a measure of the extinguisher "charge." For real safety, never buy one that is not approved by Underwriters' Laboratories, Inc. Then, have it tested and refilled every year (or two, as recommended on the label).

Some other fire-safety hints: If you should have a grease fire or even heavy smoking on your cooktop or range, DO NOT turn on the hood fan. That would increase the draft. Too, if the filter has not been washed recently, there is danger of it catching fire. From there the fire could spread into your attic.

For those reasons, the hood fan should always be vented through the roof to the outside. If it is vented into the attic, the dangerous accumulation of smoke-borne grease soon develops a spontaneous-combustion hazard in the attic.

One last safety hint (there are other, more specific ones all through the book). If you don't have a high shelf or locked cabinet for storing caustic cleaning supplies (sink cleaner, rust remover, bowl cleaner, bleach, and ammonia), build one. Small children drink almost any liquid they find, completely ignoring offensive odors or tastes. They may or may not attempt to eat dry material, but just as bad is the danger of getting it on their hands and rubbing it in their eyes.

Pressurized cans, gasoline, kerosene, and insecticides should also be stored out of reach—and NOT in the kitchen near heat as shown here.

Chapter 2

A Right Way to Do Things

Home repairs can be simple if you have the right tools and know how to use them. The photo below shows the pile of basic tools accumulated by one typical homeowner. Some are fine; others could be better. Either way, your real success depends on how well you use the tools you have. This chapter helps you recognize good tools and shows you how to learn as painlessly as possible to use them. Only the most basic tools are covered; further along in the book you'll see specialized tools for particular jobs.

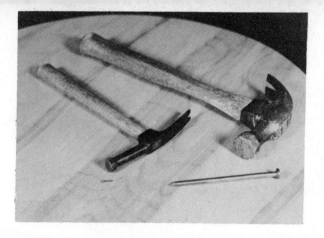

Take the hammer as a starter. Just any old hammer won't do. Cheap hammers are often out of balance, making it all but impossible to drive a nail straight. You bend nails, mash fingers, damage woodwork. Buy a well balanced hammer, preferably with a husky wood handle that fits your hand. Assure yourself that the hammering surface is perfectly (machined) flat. The faintest rounding prevents accurate hammering.

You'll probably need two hammers. A big one can drive eight-penny (8d) and larger nails. For tacks, brads, and finishing nails, buy a smaller hammer; the large one gets too clumsy.

DON'T "CHOKE" the hammer. Holding the handle too close to the head introduces disadvantages. First, you just don't have leverage to swing the hammer in a businesslike way. Timid pecking bends nails. Second, the choked grip leads to wobbly strokes, again resulting in nails bent whenever the hammer glances off the nail head.

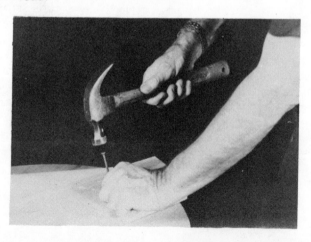

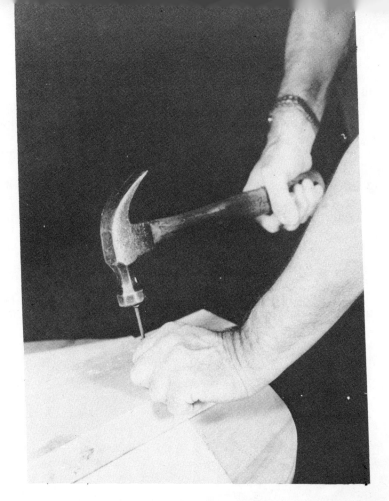

Here's how to hold a hammer. Use a good, tight "fist" grip, near the end of the handle. This isn't easy for the beginner. But learn to do it this way. Correct hammering takes firm, unhesitant strokes. With only a little practice, you can drive a nail as consistently as any carpenter.

There are two steps to driving a nail accurately. The first, illustrated here, is *setting* the nail. Align the wood and fix it so neither piece can move. Use clamps if you must. Then, grip the hammer as already described (no "choking" here either). With the other hand, place the tip of the nail in exactly the right spot. The nail should be exactly upright (or tilted very slightly away from you—more about this on the following page). Using a "bounce" stroke, tap the nail lightly until it is far enough into the wood to support itself steadily.

Once the nail is securely set, get your fingers away. Pound the nail "home" with firm, long, vertical stokes of the hammer. Get some elbow action into the hammering. Wrist action does okay for setting the nail, but it takes both wrist and elbow to get a solid driving stroke.

In your first attempts to drive a nail this way, you'll hit the head off-center and bend the nail a few times. That's the cost of learning. Don't revert to the timid, hesitating way. Act as if you mean it. Very quickly, you'll learn to pound nails accurately. If you continue the "gentle" way of driving a nail, you'll never really learn to do it right.

Some carpenters lean the nail away very slightly as they set it, in order to get a straight drive. Others set the nail straight. Experiment a few times with some old lumber to learn what angle gets you a straight drive. You do not want the nail to go through the boards at an angle (except for special construction purposes not covered here). Your own technique will depend to some extent on your particular arm-swing and wrist action. At the start, you might best set the nail straight, and then develop your own setting slant as you gain experience.

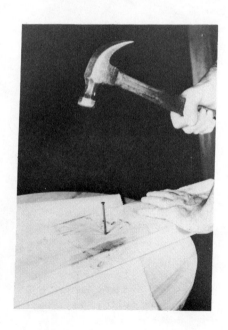

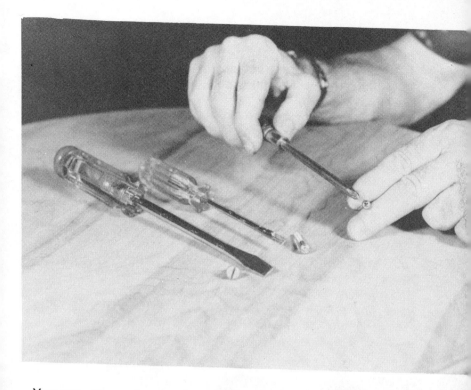

You may know already that home repairs takes two kinds of screwdrivers: regular and Phillips. The Phillips fits screws with recessed, crossed slots. Phillips screws generally drive into wood easier than ordinary screws. What screw to use for which purpose is beyond this book, which is devoted to quick and practical repairs rather than to building projects. The rule-of-thumb for repairs is: Replace with the same kind of screw already being used in whatever you're repairing. (Sometimes you'll need a slightly larger size, as you will see further along in the book.)

Screwdrivers are not expensive, so don't buy cheap ones. Choose plastic handles. You'll want at least two sizes of regular screwdriver and one Phillips. Buy to fit the sizes of screws you deal with most. To use a too-small bit quickly damages the head slots.

When a screwdriver gets worn, replace it. You can "sharpen" a regular screwdriver by grinding the end of the bit square when it gets worn. But unless you know what you're doing, you may destroy the metal temper and it'll wear out again quickly.

If you must replace a screw that no longer grips, and therefore leaves the joint loose, the common procedure is to use a screw that's slightly longer and perhaps slightly larger in diameter. Take the old one with you to the hardware store for comparison. But there's a better way.

Whenever possible, use a new screw of the original size and find a new place to put it, where the wood isn't split or cracked or deteriorated. If you go about it right, the new screw won't crack or split the wood and the joint will have all its original strength (or more).

In one piece of the wood, drill a guide hole for the screw. The hole diameter must be slightly smaller than the size of the screw. The second piece of wood, into which the tip of the screw goes, should also be drilled, but only to about half the depth the screw will reach. (About two-fifths of the screw's length should go into the second piece of wood.) Use a slightly smaller drill bit to make the "bottom" screw hole. These guide holes also let the screw enter the wood without spreading the wood fibers enough to cause splitting and strain on the joint.

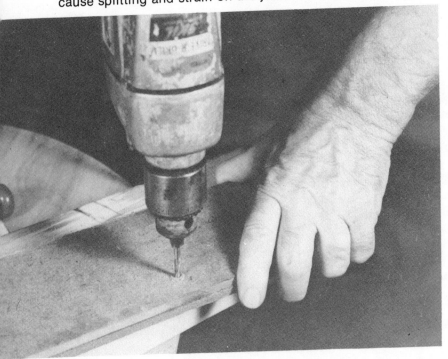

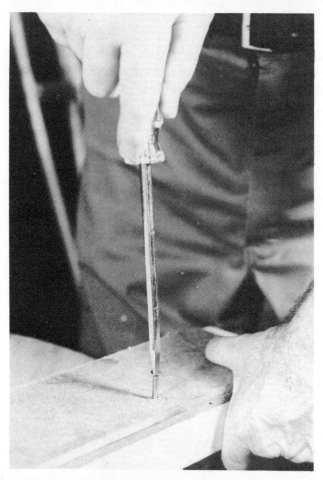

Install the screw with a screwdriver that fits the slot properly. The right size of screwdriver can't slip out and leave burrs that are unsightly and ruin the screw head. If the guide holes are drilled as they should be, the screw goes into the joint snugly and firmly. It shouldn't take enormous pressure on the screwdriver to turn the screw, nor should it turn too easily. When the screw is almost all the way in, then it should begin turning tightly; otherwise the bottom hole has been drilled too deep. There's not much you can do about it then, but the joint won't be solid unless the new screw gets a solid "bite" of wood.

Tighten the screw until the head is down snug against the wood. If the screw head has a flat top, drive it in until the flat top is flush with the wood surface. Rounded-head screws should tighten down just snug against the surface.

Sawing often becomes an important part of home repairs. Not many beginners know how to saw properly. First of all, of course, you buy a good-quality handsaw. Don't buy the small-size cheap ones. They don't saw well, they bend easily, and they don't hold their "set" well—they have to be resharpened too often. Take your saw once a year for setting and sharpening, anyway. It's not too expensive and few tools are as ineffective as a bent or dull saw.

Draw a line on the piece of lumber to be sawed, to guide your cut. (See opposite page for use of a square.) Then clamp the work in a woodworking vise or at least place it on a bench or table that is not wobbly. A table or sawhorse should hold the work at about hip-pocket level. Find a way to hold the work steady. Any wobble or shake makes it tough to saw straight.

Aim the saw at about a 45-degree angle, and apply the pull and push in that direction. Don't "push downward" on the saw to speed sawing. Just run it back and forth in the slot that forms. The weight of the saw will do the work if the saw is sharp.

Near the end of the cut, catch the free end of the wood, so its weight doesn't split off part of the sawed piece and leave an unsightly corner.

In most instances, it's important to get a saw-cut square. The implement for guiding that is the carpenter's square. You can buy small inexpensive ones, but even a large one is not very costly. The longer the square is, the more accurate you can be. Most squares include inch markings, useful for measuring as well as for laying out angles.

Sometimes you need to be able to make and saw an exact 45-degree angle on a board, such as for mitering a corner (where two pieces of lumber fit together neatly at right angles, such as at the corner of a picture frame). A "mitering box" is best, but some kinds of small squares include a 45-degree angle along with the 90-degree. (The one shown below also has a built-in leveling bubble—see page 31.)

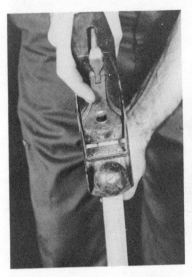

You will have occasion to use a carpenter's plane for some repairs. There are several sizes. Buy the medium size. Then, as with any other cutting tool, keep it sharp. You can't properly sharpen a blade for your plane, even if you have a bench grinder. The angle of sharpening is critical. The fee is minor, and the blade will only need it every year or two unless you use the plane a lot.

Always plane *with* the grain of wood. You cannot plane anything successfully across the grain. The photos on this page show how to hold the tool for most planing. If you have a bench vise to hold the work, you can use both hands on the plane. As with sawing, though, do not mash downward. Let the weight of the plane determine how much it "cuts." It'll work fine that way if the blade is sharp. The job will look "gouged" if you force the planing.

You sometimes have to determine if a wall or door-facing is plumb (exactly vertical) or if a floor or step is perfectly level. A carpenter's level is the tool. Don't buy a short one. The longer the better. It should have two bubble tubes, at right angles to each other for checking both plumb and level. Used as shown in these photos, the instrument's two bubbles show whether a wall, support post, ceiling joist, bench, or whatever, is aligned exactly vertical or horizontal. The bubble centers at the black line on the bubble tube whenever level or plumb is correct.

When leveling is wrong, the bubble always is off-center toward whichever end is too high. When plumb is wrong, the bubble is off-center *opposite* to whatever direction the *top* of the wall or post leans.

Possibly the most useful of several kinds of pliers you might buy are "slip-joint" or Channellock pliers. They are adjustable to fit a wide variety of nuts, bolts, pipes, etc. The handles are long, giving you a strong grip when it's necessary. As usual, though, DO NOT buy a cheap pair, or you'll be shopping again before very long.

There are specific ways to use such pliers. For example, keep your fingers and thumbs out from between the handles; if the jaws slip, the pinch you would get can be painful.

Always apply turning pressure to the handles in a way that tends to close the jaws, thus making them hold the object tighter. For example, in the photo, pressure should be downward since the jaws are "pointed" downward. If you need for some reason to pull upward, reverse the pliers to turn the jaws upward. If you notice, that means you *always* apply pressure to the handle that connects to the underside or shorter jaw of the pliers. This habit will save you considerable skinned knuckles and you won't foul up as many nuts, boltheads, or whatever you're trying to tighten or loosen.

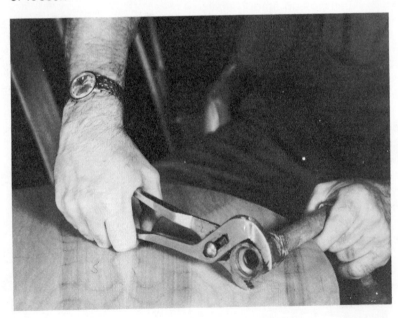

Chapter 3

Keeping the Kitchen Running

If you set out really to keep your house in a fine state of repair, a lot of your efforts will be spent in the kitchen. In most homes, that's the work center. Most of the appliances are there and in the basement (or utility room). Consequently, there simply is more to break down or to need periodic attention.

This chapter is not a manual for appliance repair. Yet, you can save a surprising amount of money every year if you can make certain rudimentary repairs to kitchen appliances and fixtures yourself. Too, with an informed eye, you can spot many potential troubles before they reach the costly stage, and can call in a professional service expert before a minor problem turns into a major repair job.

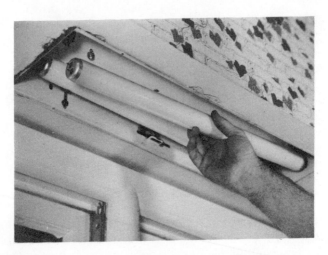

Lighting probably is the most basic kitchen need. Most modern kitchens have fluorescent lights because they throw such shadowless and efficient illumination.

Fluorescent tubes last much longer than incandescent bulbs. But they do eventually wear out. Usually, they start flickering, and you can see where the inner coating is flaking off near the ends.

In older fixtures, the tubes have two prongs on each end. The prongs fit into slots in holders at each end of the fixture. To remove a tube, give it a quarter-turn either way and it will drop right out of the holders. (Sometimes there's a plastic cover to remove before you have access to fluorescent fixtures recessed in the ceiling. Just slide the cover sideways and/or lift one side or end.)

To put in a new tube, line up the prongs with the slots in both ends of the fixture. Push the prongs up into the slot and give the tube a quarter-turn.

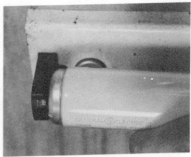

In newer fixtures, a one-prong fluorescent tube is used. Nearly all longer fixtures, from four-foot lengths on up, use this type of tube because it is so much easier to change the tube. The fixtures have holders at each end, one of which has a spring assembly inside. Removing a tube like this requires that you push it farther into that holder and carefully lower the other end of the tube till it is free of its holder.

To replace this type of tube, just reverse the action. Push one end of the tube into the holder with the spring assembly and press until the other end of the tube can fit into the holder at that end of the fixture.

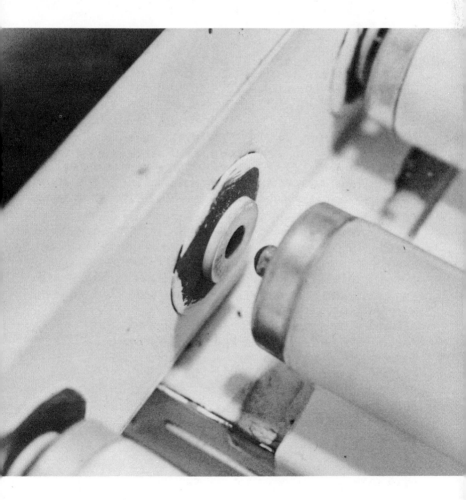

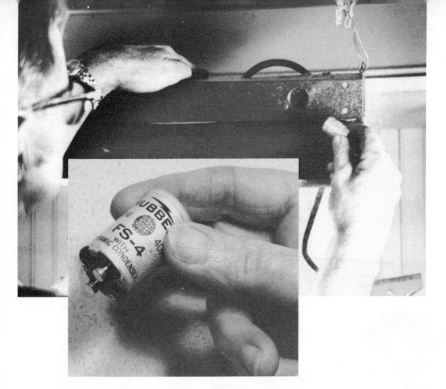

Newer fluorescent fixtures have instant-start transformers, but older fixtures have what are called starters. This little device warms up the gases in the fluorescent tube before full voltage is applied.

Suppose you have a flickering or unlit fluorescent tube. You'd probably try a new tube first. But if a new tube doesn't light, replace the starter. You may find it above the fluorescent tube, or it may be behind the fixture. If it is above the tube (as shown at the bottom of page 34)), you will have to remove the tube before you can get it out.

Give the old starter a quarter-turn to the left and pull it out. Take the starter to your electrical supplier and get a new one just like it. Press the new starter into the socket and give it a quarter turn to the right to lock it in.

A noisy hum in fluorescent lights usually calls for a new transformer. This is not a job for you. Call an electrician.

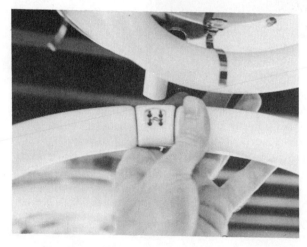

Rather common nowadays in kitchens is the round fluorescent light fixture. It takes a special circular fluorescent tube.

Many experts suggest trying a new starter before you change a fluorescent tube. (This applies only to fluorescent fixtures that use a starter.) The reasoning is that starters are more trouble-prone. They say you should keep an extra around as a spare. The fact is, you should also have one spare of each type fluorescent tube you use. They're not too costly and a flickering fluorescent can be very hard on your eyesight.

Turning to your kitchen appliances, the refrigerator and stove usually are next in line for consideration. The refrigerator generally demands the most attention. Here are some suggestions to save you money in this area of the kitchen.

If your refrigerator door has a tendency not to close by itself, you can waste electricity and food if it is accidentally left standing open. When that happens, the refrigerator needs leveling. You'll find the leveling screws, one on either side, near the front corners below the door. There usually is an ornamental grille or panel across the front. Just lift and snap that off.

Put some water in the bottom of a glass and set it on one of the refrigerator shelves. That will help you tell when you get the refrigerator level. Turn the screw at one corner or another in or out until refrigerator is level. Then raise the corner nearest the hinge of the refrigerator door a bit farther. The door, left standing straight out, should swing gently closed of its own accord.

Does your refrigerator run a lot, yet not seem cold enough? Check the door seal. This rubber gasket is part of the door. It is meant to seal the compartment air-tight when the door is closed. That prevents warm air from getting in, and cold air from leaking out.

If the gasket is in poor condition—worn, torn, or cracked—it cannot maintain the seal. One test is to insert a dollar bill at various points, close the door, and try to pull the bill out. If it comes easily, the seal is poor at that point. If the gasket needs to be replaced, call your appliance repairman. He has the special tools to do a good job. He can also check the liner the gasket closes against, to be sure that's not the fault instead of a bad gasket.

Another cause of unnatural operation might be that the temperature control is not set properly. A refrigerator control is usually marked Cold, Colder, and Coldest. The knob needs to be set colder for hot summer weather than it does for fall and winter. It should also be set for a colder temperature if you have occasion to open the door more often than usual—as perhaps when company comes.

Know where the air vents are in your refrigerator and freezer. Be careful not to let anything get pushed against the vents in a way that restricts the air flow. The cold air must be free to circulate. Otherwise, the motor runs more often than it should, and foodstuffs can't stay as evenly chilled as they must for safe storage.

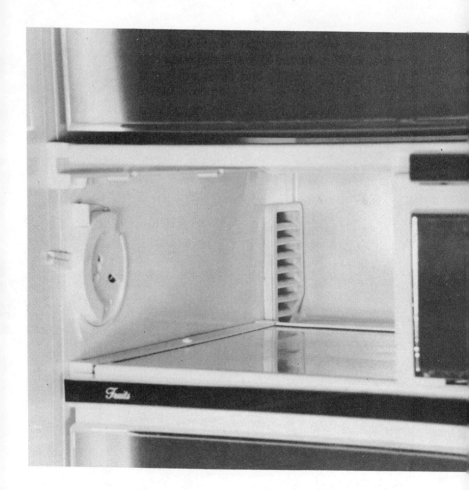

You've probably heard that if the milk stays good and cold the refrigerator is cold enough. Or that if ice cream keeps, the freezer is okay. These sayings could be so, but what if you don't keep milk or ice cream?

It's better anyway to own a refrigerator and freezer thermometer and play it safe. The temperature in your refrigerator should not stray above 40 degrees. It's even better for the food between 35 and 39 degrees.

Freezer temperature should not rise above zero degrees. Foods that are being stored for several months keep their flavor better at 10 degrees or so below zero.

Avoid crowding food into your freezer (lefthand photo). For proper cooling and even temperature in the freezer, the air has to circulate freely over and around every package and container.

It's better to put less in the freezer (righthand photo). That way, what food you do keep will look better and taste better when you prepare it for the table. Foods do not spoil in the freezer, in the common meaning of the word; but they can deteriorate and lose flavor and texture if they're not stored properly. A loose arrangement offers freer flow of cold air.

Another detriment to freezer operation is an accumulation of frost. It actually acts as an insulator and prevents efficient cooling.

Don't be tempted to hurry the task of getting frost off the freezer unit with an ice pick when you defrost the freezer. The cooling agent is a gas that circulates through a system of small tubes. The tubes lay right against the unit and extend over and around it. If the freezer unit has a shelf for ice-cube trays, some of the gas tubes are fastened to this shelf. In newer models, the tubes may even be molded into the aluminum of the shelf and freezing-compartment liner.

If you wield an ice pick, you run the risk of puncturing one or more of these tubes. That releases the gas. Closing the leak and replacing the refrigerant constitutes a major repair.

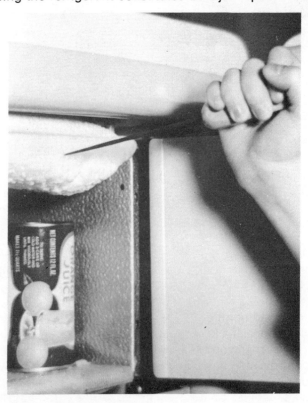

If your cooktop or range has push-button controls, make sure the control button for the burner you wish to use is pushed in firmly. Otherwise, it does not make good contact. You get poor or improper heating.

The same admonition holds for rotary burner switches. They have click-stops. If a knob happens to be left carelessly between clicks, the burner won't be connected right for the heat you want. If the controls are out front, below the burners at waist level, it is easy to brush against them accidentally when reaching for something in a cabinet or on a shelf above the cooktop. This can depress pushbuttons about halfway, causing them to disconnect the burner. Or a loose apron-pocket can twist a rotary knob.

If the burners on your electric range or cooktop barely get warm, the likely cause is a blown fuse. Your stove operates on 220 volts of electricity. That's double the regular wall-outlet voltage. This 220-volt circuit comes from a special "double" hookup at your electric service box.

Two fuses usually protect the circuit from overload. One may blow, leaving only half the circuit (a mere 110 volts) operative. The fuses are in the electric service box. If you have no way to test them, replace both fuses. They are marked 30A or 30 amp on the top. Replace them with fuses of the same ratings.

If you have a breaker-type service box, the breaker that controls voltage to your range or cooktop usually has two handles connected by a metal bar. Sometimes two entirely separate breakers are used. Flip them both back and forth. This action will reset the breakers in case one is tripped. Now try the burners.

Other malfunctions can cause a burner to heat poorly. Or, you may find one of the burners not heating at all. Turn off the MAIN power switch at your electric service box. (Remember, you saw this switch on page 11.) This makes the stove safe to handle electrically.

Remove the burner by lifting one side up and out. That reveals the screws that hold the wires that carry voltage to the burner. Check for loose, frayed, or burned-off wires. If the connections are loose, tighten them by turning the screws clockwise with a screwdriver. It helps remove accumulated corrosion if you twist the screw back and forth a few times before tightening.

If a wire is burned off, cut away the burned end. Remove enough insulation from the end of the remaining wire so it will fit under the screw. Either apply solder to hold the strands together or attach a ring-type terminal lug (similar to the spade lug described on page 16). Fasten the wires solidly to their proper terminals on the burner. Put the burner back together. Restore power at the Main switch. If the burner still does not heat, you may have a bad stove switch or the wiring is damaged or miswired. Call your appliance repair technician.

If your range uses gas and the burners don't heat properly, the first thing to check is the gas source. If you use bottled (LP) gas, see if the bottle is empty. Connected to city gas supply? Check the turn-on valve at the meter and/or behind the stove.

If the burners are lazy, or not burning all over, some of the little jets have probably gotten stopped up. This often happens when something boils over or gets spilled on the burner.

Remove the burner and plop it into a kettle of water to which you have added a pint of vinegar. Boil for about fifteen minutes. Then wash the burner in soapy or detergent water. Use a scrub brush to remove any remaining traces of burned-on food. Rinse, let dry, and replace.

If your oven refuses to heat, make sure the automatic and manual controls are properly set. You may have used the timed baking controls and forgot. Or someone else may have messed with them. With these controls, the oven is controlled automatically by the clock. They turn off the oven at a certain time. Unless they are reset, you cannot turn the oven on manually. Beyond simple checks such as this and perhaps replacing a burned-out light bulb (Appliance 40-watt is the type), call your repair expert.

Inside the hood over the cooktop or range, you will find a grease filter (mentioned on page 19 in connection with fire safety). This filter should be removed and scrubbed thoroughly with hot, soapy water—at least once a month. If grease is allowed to accumulate, the filter can no longer do a good job of keeping grease out of the vent pipes or attic. That also ruins efficiency of the ventilating fan. Air can no longer pull freely through the filter.

Anytime you find smoke and fumes from cooking filling the kitchen, you have already waited too long for this cleanup.

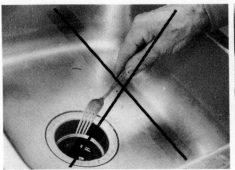 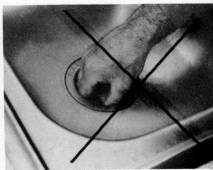

Garbage-disposal troubles usually fall into two categories: (1) just won't turn on, and (2) jammed. The first is caused by a bad switch, an open fuse or circuit breaker, or a faulty motor. You can replace fuses or reset a breaker. But if the unit keeps overloading and tripping off, call the repair technician. He should take care of bad switches or burned-out motors.

If the garbage-disposal jams, you can try to fix that. Be very careful, though. A tool to free such jams is supplied with most garbage disposals. If you have it—use it. DO NOT reach in with your fingers. Do not use forks, knives, or spoons as a tool. Remember you are dealing with a powerful grinder that doesn't know the difference between your fingers and the garbage it is supposed to chew up.

A homemade notched wooden probe is just about as efficient as any tool to get the grinder jaws moving again. The object is to get the mechanism to release whatever has caused the jam. Be sure the disposal motor is turned off. Reach in with the notched probe and try to push the grinder to the left or counterclockwise. (The mechanism turns clockwise when it is operating.) A little jiggling, and you may shake loose the bone or whatever stopped the grinder's action. Turn on the switch to check.

Automatic dishwashers can give you fits sometimes. It's frustrating to have such a handy appliance if it doesn't work. When it's completely inoperative, there are several things you can check before you give up and call the repairman.

Have you overstacked it? Some of the silverware might have slipped down into the mechanism and blocked the spinning water jet. Of course you would have already checked fuses and circuit breakers, to make sure electric power reaches the machine. After you've checked such seemingly obvious possibilities, try running the control knob through its several "steps" manually by hand. Maybe part of the complex switch doesn't function. Troubles like that are a job for a repair specialist.

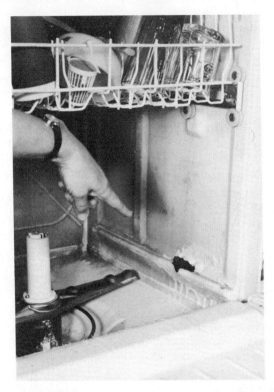

How do you know what kind of repairman to call? Generally, a dishwasher technician can take care of both plumbing and electrical problems—unless the trouble lies definitely outside the dishwasher itself. If no electricity reaches the dishwasher, the cure lies in the realm of an electrician. By the same token, if water doesn't reach the input tubing of the dishwasher, the problem must be corrected by a plumber. If you're lucky enough to have a generalist type of repair expert, he can track down the trouble wherever it is and make the fix.

A waste-water outlet line may block somewhere, causing a backup that leaves the dishwasher full of dirty water. That's a plumber's job. A backup like this can eventually ruin the liner, if allowed to persist. The liner could develop breaks that show up as rusty spots (where rust from the outside leaks through). The plumber must clear the drain blockage, and your dishwasher man should patch or replace the liner.

If your dishwasher does not get dishes clean, there are several things to check out. Do you have good water pressure? Have you stacked the dishes properly? Are you using a dishwasher detergent? An instruction panel inside the door usually tells you the right way to arrange dishes in the washer. If you wash dishes once a day instead of after every meal, they need to be rinsed before you stack them in the dishwasher. See if the detergent cup cover is free. Don't stack any large dish or utensil where it will, when the door is closed, prevent water circulating properly over the cup. That would let the detergent cake and clog the cup.

If you live in a hard-water area, you may find spots remaining on glassware and silver after they have washed and dried. A product called Jet-Dry will help eliminate this spotting. Jet-Dry comes in individual open-wick plastic cups. You just hang one on the top rack in the dishwasher. Leave it there until it's empty. A small amount is released each time the dishes are washed.

Before we leave the subject of kitchen appliances, you should know the fairly simple things you can check with *all* appliances before you telephone for a repair technician.

(1) Make sure the appliance that refuses to run is plugged in. This may seem too simple a solution to mention, but it happens—for any number of reasons.

(2) Be sure the switch is turned on. Even a repair expert can slip up on this one.

(3) Always check fuses and circuit breakers. If they blow or trip repeatedly, you will need a repair technician (or an electrician if no faulty appliance is overloading the circuits).

These seem like obvious hints, but they still represent the most common "nuisance" calls service shops get.

Of course, appliances are not the only kitchen objects that require repairs. Chairs, tables, and cabinets need attention. Some repairs are deceptively simple.

For example, maybe you have a kitchen chair that is wobbly and coming apart. Turn it upside down and tighten the screws clockwise with a screwdriver (one that fits the screwheads). If one or two screws are missing, take one of those remaining to the hardware store, and buy enough of the same size and length (or very slightly larger) to replace them all.

Shoddy workmanship goes into some furniture these days. It pays to inspect all kitchen chairs, even new ones, every six months and keep them tightened up *before* they get wobbly. You may even discover that screws used to put the chair together at the factory are not really long enough for the stress of normal use. If you find them working loose regularly, buy some longer ones and fasten the chair together properly.

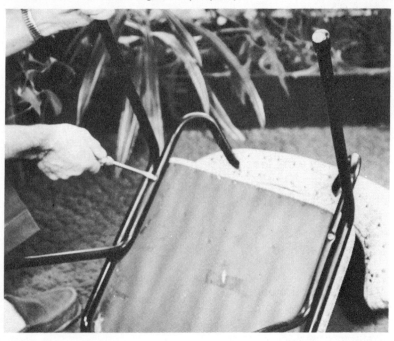

Dinette tables, particularly the less expensive kind with tubular aluminum legs, frequently become shaky or completely disabled. Screws that hold the legs to the fiberboard or Masonite subsurface of the tabletop work loose. They may even drop out and be swept away unnoticed.

You'll find three conditions. First and most common, the screws merely work loose. Periodic attention takes care of this kind of wobble. Turn the table up on its side once a year and tighten each screw. Don't force any of them, as the threads strip easily in the Masonite.

The second condition: missing screws. Take one of the remaining screws out and go buy additional ones exactly the same size and length. If the missing screw wasn't pulled or torn out, thus stripping the hole, you can merely insert a new screw and tighten.

You find the third condition when a table has been misused or is old and rickety. Some of the screws have stripped out. New ones can't get a firm "bite." The solution lies in moving the legs slightly to one side or inward from their original positions. You can reposition one leg or all of them. New screws driven into fresh holes in the Masonite can tighten up a table you might otherwise throw away.

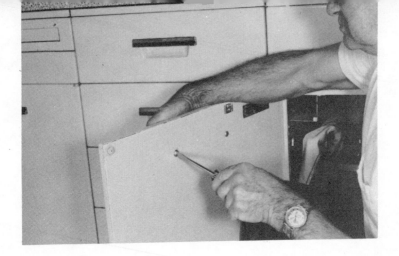

You can dress up your kitchen and add new life to it. Remove the pulls from all drawers and cabinets. These pulls are usually fastened with screws from the inside. The screws go through holes in the door or drawer front and into the handles, which have matching threads in each end. Hold the handle with one hand and remove the screws with a screwdriver, turning counterclockwise.

Take the screws to your hardware store and buy new ones of the same size and threads but cadmium-plated. When you finish with the "dressup" described on the facing page, use these rustproof screws (bolts) to fasten the handles back to the cabinets and drawers. That gives a more permanent job.

There usually are worn and/or rusty spots around the handles. Take fine sandpaper and sand them until the blemishes and the surfaces around them feel smooth to the touch. The sanding is important, if you are to avoid a rough spot that looks bad after you finish. Clean off the sanding-dust.

Paint the sanded areas first with enamel undercoat, and let dry several hours or overnight. THEN, paint all the cabinets and drawers with the same enamel undercoat. This helps cover old paint, and gives the places that were sanded a second coat. (See pages 124–125 for more hints about painting.)

After the undercoat is thoroughly dry, apply a coat of enamel in whatever color adds sparkle and zest to your kitchen.

Cabinets with loose drawer pulls take but a few minutes to tighten. Look inside the drawer. The pulls are fastened on with a bolt or with a nut assembly. Hold the pull with one hand to keep it from turning. Take a pair of pliers and turn the nut clockwise to tighten it. If a bolt goes through the drawer-front into the pull (as on the two preceding pages), use a screwdriver.

Chapter 4

The Operations Center: Basement or Utility Room

Almost all the appurtenances that keep your household operating are fitted into your basement or utility room. Depending on where you live, these may include furnace, central air conditioning, water pump and storage tank, water softener, water heater, sump pump, and usually such appliances as washer and dryer.

For all this home-operating "machinery," you should devise a schedule of regular maintenance. Few homeowners ever do this. But, if you were to take the trouble, you could derive three major benefits: (1) Breakdowns would occur less frequently, thus avoiding inconvenience and wasted dollars in equipment "down time." (2) Equipment would last years longer, thus saving many dollars of replacement expense. (3) Outages that do occur would be less severe and would therefore cost less in repair bills.

The following pages offer some additional ways to cut down maintenance costs through your own repair efforts.

Whether your furnace burns oil or gas, it needs periodic atten- tion. When you call a heating technician to do the maintenance work, he should adjust air and fuel flow, oil the blowers, and clean the furnace throughout. He even cleans the air ducts, if neces- sary. All this assures greatest efficiency, economy, and heating from your fuel dollar.

The best time to have this work done is during the summer months. Maintenance people are not as busy then. An appoint- ment that lets the heating service company schedule work at their most convenient time may get you a better price. Ask, anyway.

Naturally, the furnace breaks down most often during the first spell of cold weather. If you wait till that happens, you may find the service people so busy you are put on a waiting list. That could be a long, cold wait.

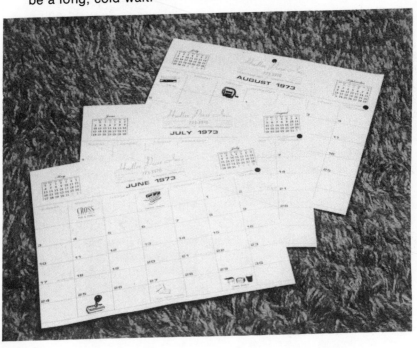

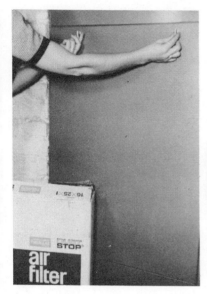

When the technician services your furnace, he will change the air filter. But the filter needs changing more than once per season, especially during coldest weather when the furnace runs most. All the warmed air that heats your house passes through this filter (or filters) as it goes through the ducts in your hot-air system. A dirty, clogged filter allows only poor heating because air finds it difficult to circulate freely through the filter.

Have the servicer show you where the filter is located. The position varies with different brands of furnaces. Some furnaces use two filters.

Filters come in many different sizes. When you remove the old one, look along the edge. Printed in large numbers, you will see the correct size for your furnace.

Most neighborhood hardware stores carry filters in the popular sizes. If they don't have the right size for your furnace, you can get a half-dozen from your heating service headquarters.

You will find an arrow, or arrows, on the side of the filter. That indicates the direction of air flow. Install the new filter with the arrows pointing in the direction the blower pushes the air through the ducts. (Don't always trust the old filter orientation; someone may have put it in backward.)

If you like a nice, warm house, make sure nothing restricts the flow of warm air from your registers. Be sure floor registers are free of all floor coverings. These cautions apply to the opening for cold-air-return ducts, too. Hot-air heating depends on circulation of air throughout the house.

With wall registers, be careful in placing furniture. Even a window drape can interfere with air flow. You can't expect the furnace to push warm air through a solid piece of furniture.

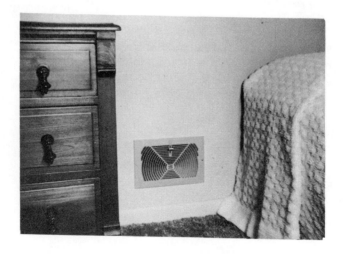

You may have heard claims that one type of heating fuel is cleaner than another. There may be some small differences. But there's one really good way to keep the house cleaner during heating season: frequent vacuuming of the heating and cold-air-return registers. Just use the vacuum-cleaner with hose attachment.

Any forced-air heating system picks up dust, lint, and smoke. What gets past the filters just naturally circulates throughout the house. The cold-air-return ducts tend to attract dust from room air. Much of this debris gets caught on the registers. This condition lowers heating efficiency because it interferes with free circulation of air.

You already know (from Chapter 2) some of the tricks to dealing with cantankerous electric appliances in kitchens. Here are some more aids regarding utility appliances like washers and dryers.

Aid number one: READ THE INSTRUCTION MANUAL. One is provided with each new appliance you purchase. Keep them all filed so you can refer to them when you need to. These booklets tell you how to use all the controls on your appliance, explain what each control is meant to do, and warn of things you should not do.

Typical example: Never turn an appliance control backward. This interferes with the mechanism and may throw the unit out of adjustment.

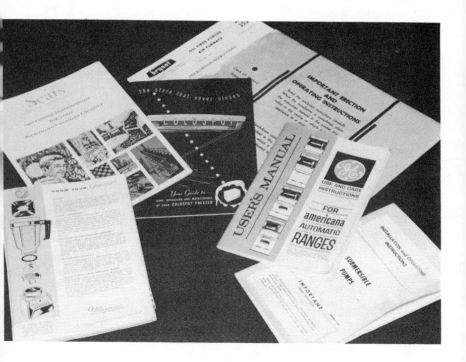

Be sure all controls are set properly for the job you want to do. In the more sophisticated washing machines, you must select the right water temperature, the correct speed, and the washing-cycle time for the type of load you are washing. All of these controls are plainly labeled, but you must know what the labels actually mean. After you get them set, the machine should go through its cycle without any more attention.

See that the door of the appliance is closed and latched. Many will not run with doors left open. Usually, this is a safety measure. Washing machines can't go into the spin cycle, and the dryer won't tumble, until the door is closed and latched. Hence, no harm could come to a small child who might crawl inside one of the machines. (The circulating fan in a frost-free refrigerator does not run when the door is open. It would increase the outflow of cold air.)

If clothes drying takes longer than normal, the lint screen can be clogged. Clean the lint catcher after each load to assure free circulation of air. The dryer could overheat dangerously, otherwise. Also consult the dryer manual so you don't exceed the load capacity (too many clothes) for your machine.

Sooner or later your appliance will need professional help. Find the model number and give that to the repair technician when you call. Explain as well as you can how the appliance is malfunctioning. Describe odd noises, overheating, or in a washing machine at what stage of the cycle it quit operating.

When the technician arrives, get the kids and pets out of the room, and you stay out of his way too.

With a growing preference for noncity living, you may have your own well and water system. Some problems that occur, you wouldn't have with city water. Loss of pressure is typical.

It is important to have the right amount of air in your cold-water storage tank. This affects the water pressure in your system. To test it, run just one glass of water. If that makes the pump start, your tank is waterlogged—full of water and no air.

At the electric service box, take out the fuse or open the breaker that serves your water pump. Drain the tank. Most cold-water storage tanks have a drain cock at the bottom where you can attach a hose. Close the drain after the tank is empty.

There's a place you can pump air in. Use an old-fashioned hand pump (unless you have a compressor). Put in enough air to build up about 15 pounds of pressure.

Put the fuse back in, or close the breaker. The pump should kick in immediately. If not, the pressure switch might be faulty. The pump fills the tank with water. The combination of air- and water-pressure should build up to 40/60 pounds before the pump shuts off. The system now should maintain good water pressure over reasonable use loads.

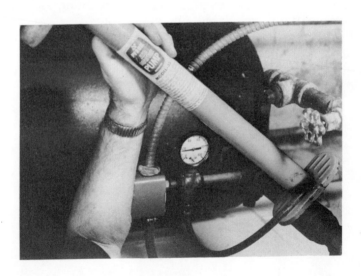

Chapter 5

Be Your Own Plumber

Don't panic if something goes wrong with your plumbing. You can fix quite a few of the common difficulties yourself. You'll need only relatively simple tools: a pair of adjustable pliers, an adjustable (Crescent) wrench, a screwdriver, and a "plumber's friend" or rubber plunger. Of course with certain problems you would need some extra tools. There are tool-renting establishments in nearly every town, and several in larger towns. You can rent special tools for almost any repair job you know how to do.

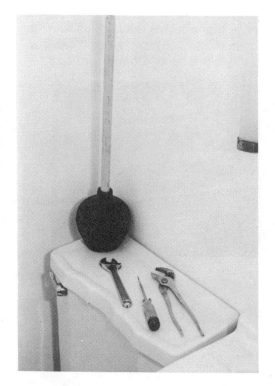

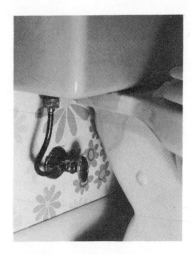

A good way to start, if you want to do your own plumbing repairs, is through familiarization with the plumbing in your house. Make an inventory of all your water-line shutoff valves. Ordinarily there is one under each water fixture. This shutoff comes in handy in emergencies such as a busted faucet or an overflowing toilet tank.

They are even more useful when you have to make repairs. You may have to hunt for the one that governs the bathtub faucets. This shutoff may be in a linen closet or tucked away in a cubby-hole of its own. However, it will not be far from the faucets.

It is not recommended practice, but some plumbers take short-cuts. You may find that whoever put in your system did not install individual shutoff valves at each fixture location. When you need to make repairs, you will have to shut off the water for the whole house, at the main supply valve. This is located near where the water line enters the house.

In rare instances, the only shutoff is outside at the water meter. If that's the case in your house, have a professional plumber come install a master shutoff valve. You'll need it.

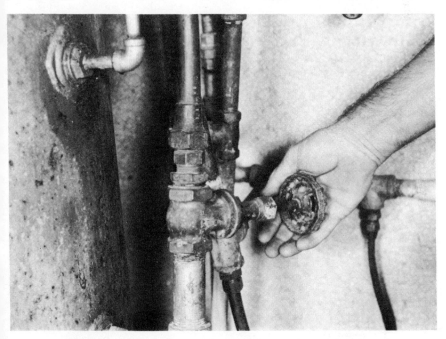

The hot-water heater may be in the basement or utility room—or in a utility closet, if your house is built on a slab.

When the water barely gets warm in an electric water heater, check for a burned-out fuse. Look in the electric service box. Two 30-amp fuses or circuit breakers protect the heater circuits. The water heater operates on 220 volts, as an electric range does (page 46). Replace both fuses, or reset the breakers by flipping them to Off and then to On.

If the water still does not heat properly, call your appliance repair technician. The difficulty could be a bad heating element or a malfunctioning thermostat.

The heater usually does its job quietly, efficiently, and without noise. If you hear noises emanating from it, chances are that something has gone wrong. The heater needs attention.

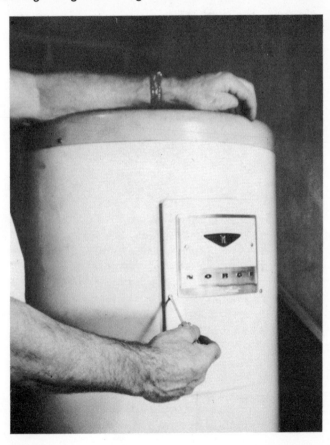

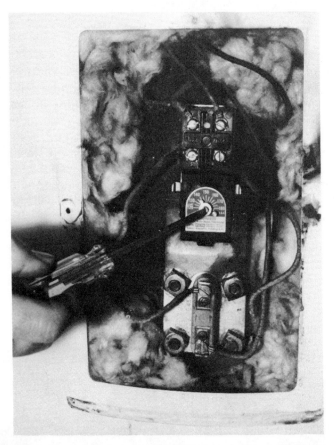

Start by checking the thermostat. Look for a small plate on the side of the water heater, fastened with two screws. Take out the screws and remove the plate. You may have to pull out a handful or two of insulation to get at the thermostat.

About 150 degrees is more than hot enough for water temperature. Never let it remain over 160 degrees. Set the temperature screw to 140 degrees and see if that stops the noise pretty soon. Occasionally the heat-control thermostat gets stuck and lets the water in the tank overheat. It may even boil. Unless you notice unusually hot water coming out of the faucets, your first warning may be the safety valve (in the top of the tank) blowing out. Then you may hear the rumble and hiss of water boiling in the tank. TURN OFF the electric circuit that leads to the water heater. (Pull fuses or flip breakers to Off.) Call a plumber.

Another noise, very noticeable, occurs sometimes when you turn a faucet off quickly. The action sets off a banging somewhere in the water system. It's called an air hammer. It develops if a bubble of air gets into the water system. Bleeding the system by opening all faucets at once can help. Turn them off slowly.

The problem can be aggravated by poor pipe layout when the system was installed. You can't do much about that, although you can relieve some of the excessive noise. Start in the basement or crawl space, checking the water lines. The pipes are supposed to be well supported by metal straps nailed to the floor joists. Pipes that are loose can vibrate against the beam, causing a pounding noise. A few more straps, available at plumbing-supply stores, may restore peace and quiet. Watch, too, for pipes that touch in crossing each other. You may have to wrap them with something soft.

A shaky, squeaking, squealing sound may develop when you turn a faucet on. Probably a faucet washer is broken or worn out. The audible torture of a dripping faucet comes from a washer that is worn or otherwise defective and lets water seep past it. Water sometimes leaks out around the stem and drips or runs around both faucets. That is caused by a faulty top gasket.

If you have to make a repair of this kind, first turn off the water to the fixture (see page 72). Take a screwdriver and remove the screw that holds the handle on, by turning the screw counterclockwise.

Unscrew the nut around the stem with an adjustable wrench. Turn the stem to the left and lift out the whole assembly.

You will find a flat fiber washer at the bottom of the stem. This is the one that presses into the pipe seat and shuts the water off. If that washer is worn or broken, it could cause the noise and the dripping. Also note a small O-ring or gasket up near the top of the stem. This gasket prevents water from leaking out around the stem.

If either of these two parts is defective, replace them both with new ones. Then reassemble the faucet. Turn on the main valve and watch for leaks at the faucet.

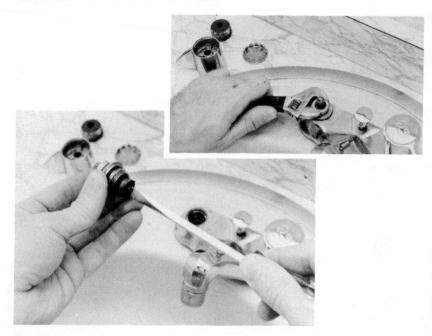

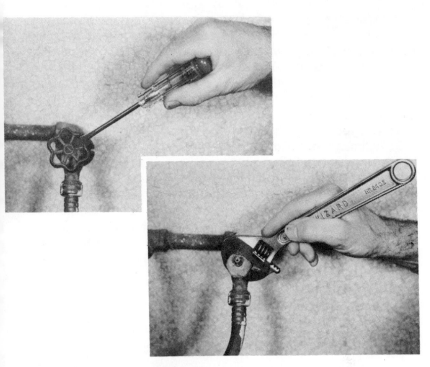

Another type of faucet has string packing around the stem. Repairing a leak around the top of it is rather simple. Remove the screw, the handle, and the nut. Take out the old, worn packing and replace it with new.

A rattle or drip can be caused by a bad washer. Take apart the stem and replace the washer in the manner already described for other type faucets. The packing and miscellaneous parts can be bought at any plumbing supply store.

Should you hear water running in the bathroom, lift the lid from the flush tank behind the toilet stool. The water level in the tank pushes a large, hollow float ball upward. Through a rod, the upward pressure closes a valve and stops water inflow after the right level is reached. If the valve doesn't close, you hear water running constantly. The tank doesn't overflow onto the floor because a standpipe beside the inflow valve carries off the excess. But you do get that annoying sound.

Sometimes the rod that connects the float to the valve gets bent. It doesn't hold the float quite low enough to close the shutoff valve completely. Bend the rod to set the float a bit further down. That should let the valve close tightly when the water level in the tank gets high enough.

If the float sinks below the water surface, it has a hole in it and is full of water. The only cure is a new one. Turn off the water at the shutoff handle under the tank, or shut off the main water valve. Hold the ball in one hand and the rod in the other. Remove the float by unscrewing it counterclockwise. Install the new one by reversing these steps.

Perhaps the tank refuses to fill with water. You can remove the valve stem by taking out the thumb screws, or wing nuts, and pushing out the bolts. This valve often gets clogged by chemical deposits from the water. Remove the stem and clean it.

Replace the washer on the bottom. Remove the small cup held on by a screw. Install the new washer under the cup.

The rubber tank-drain ball might be warped or cracked and stiff so it does not seat properly. That lets water drain into the toilet constantly. The tank can't fill up enough to shut off the inflow. If the ball lets water past, remove it from the small rod by turning counterclockwise. Replace it with a new one. Re-assemble, and turn the water supply back on.

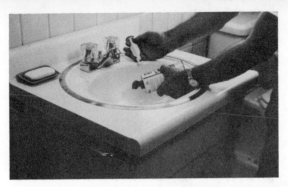

Never wait till a sink or lavatory stops draining completely to work on it. Hair or other waste easily gets wrapped around the base of the stopper. Remove the stopper: open it, give it a quarter-turn counterclockwise, and lift it out. Clean the mess off.

If drainage is still slow, wait until the water has drained away and pour in a commercial cleaner. Follow directions. These cleaners are caustic, and can damage the porcelain if left in for any time. You may, even then, need to apply the rubber plunger. Stuff a wet washcloth into overflow drain openings so the plunger can form a vacuum. Press down with the handle of the plunger and pull up sharply. Repeated several times, this should unclog the drain. But the glop may remain in the drain pipe till you remove it with "dissolving" cleaners or have a plumber do the job.

A clogged toilet drain may not yield to the foregoing measures. Small children sometimes flush a toy or other object just to see what will happen. Relieving this kind of stoppage requires a sewer tape or "snake." A long, flexible wire with a coil on the end is twisted by a crank. This tool is effective in dislodging anything that has gotten wedged in the drain.

Chapter 6

Bathroom
Repairs / Safety

It may seem strange to think of your bathroom as dangerous. But statistically, this happens to be the case. People regularly are injured seriously getting into or out of bathtubs and showers.

That's an opportunity for the home-repair expert. Add some sort of skid-proofing to the bottom of the tub or the floor of the shower stall. A rubber bath mat is good. The better ones are made with little suction cups on one side; they adhere tightly to the bottom of the tub.

Be sure. Test your bathtub mat. Run some water in the tub. Then press the suction-cup side of the mat down firmly with your hand. It should stay without any slipping.

Another type of tub skid-proofing consists of little decorative stick-on cutouts. They come in a kit, in flower or animal shapes. The back has an adhesive. To apply them, you just peel off the protective backing and press each cutout firmly to the bottom of the tub. Smooth the material well, so no air bubbles get trapped under the stick-on.

You should place a skid-proof mat or rug on the floor beside the tub. When you step out of the tub, your wet feet could otherwise slip easily on the bare floor. DO NOT use any mat that does not have slip-proof backing. It might skid when you step on it and give you a bad fall.

One very important piece of bathroom safety equipment is a grab bar. This is usually made of chrome-plated tubing. It must be attached firmly to the wall above the tub. It should be long enough and shaped so it can be reached from sitting and standing positions. It helps you get into the tub as well as out.

This piece of equipment is mandatory if elderly people live in the home. It's good insurance for everyone. If you install it, be absolutely certain the mounting screws bite into wall joists—*solid* wood—and not merely into plaster or lath.

"Don't lock bathroom doors," say safety experts. Someone who gets hurt in a fall behind a locked door is hard to reach. Yet most people want privacy. So it may become necessary to unlock a bathroom door from the outside.

Most such doors lock from the inside with a push button in the knob. They unlock automatically when you turn the knob from the inside.

The outside knob has a hole or slot in the center. A flat "key" for this lock comes with the door. Merely inserting the key unlocks the door. With a few, you have to turn the knob at the same time you insert the key into the hole or slot. If you misplace the key, a piece of stiff coathanger wire, a nail, or a slender screwdriver will work instead. Experiment a little sometime when you are not in a hurry to open the door. That way, you can discover what type of lock your bathroom door has. Then you could open it quickly in an emergency.

Hair dryers or electric razors should be used with caution in bathrooms. There's a strong shock hazard. Be sure your hands are dry and the floor is dry before you plug in appliances like these. They are usually pretty well insulated with plastic handles, but don't take any chances. Instruct every family member in these precautions.

DO NOT touch any metal faucet or pipe with wet or dry hands, nor stand barefoot on the bathroom floor, while using electrical devices. You may complete an electrical circuit with your body, resulting in severe or fatal shock.

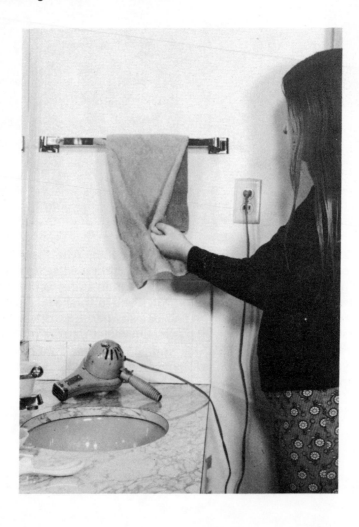

If you must have an electric heater in the bathroom for extra heat, keep it far enough away that it would be impossible to touch from the tub. There still is some danger that you could trip and fall against it while you are wet, and sustain a serious shock or burn. Too, a defective heater can "charge" a wet floor and give you a serious shock clear across the room.

It might be better to get a little chilly or bathe a little faster than to take a chance with anything so potentially lethal.

Similar precautions are necessary with a radio. If you must have music, it is safer to connect the radio outside the bathroom door or use a battery portable.

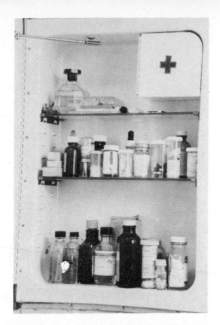

This is not repair, but it's bathroom safety. CLEAN OUT your medicine cabinet. Old prescriptions are dangerous. Changes in chemical structure and evaporation of liquids make them useless and unsafe.

Don't just dispose of old medicines in the trash. Children investigate trash barrels, and old medicines pose a threat to their health and life. Pets have also been known to sample old medicines, with dire results. The quickest and safest way: flush old medicines down the toilet. Also rinse the containers out thoroughly before pitching them into the trash.

Chapter 7

Where You Live, Loaf, and Sleep

There's no room in a house that doesn't need repairs sooner or later. In living rooms and bedrooms, as often as not it's furniture that needs the most attention. That's where you'll apply the main hints and helps in this chapter.

Let's start with reclining chairs. With age, they become hard to tip backward and forward. The difficulty may be eased by applying powdered graphite to the metal parts that rub together. You can buy a small squeeze-tube of powdered graphite at almost any lumber yard or hardware store. Graphite is far better than oil because it lubricates well without leaving a sticky residue to catch dust or drip on the floor.

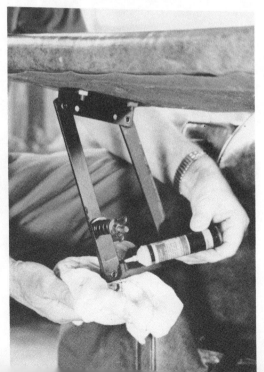

Tip the chair back and rock it back and forth a little, to help you see the places that need lubricating.

If lubrication doesn't ease the chair's movement enough, you may have to adjust the tension. Tip the chair back and look at the extension bars on both sides. On each outside bar, there's usually a wingnut. Loosen them just a little by turning counterclockwise. That should let the chair tip back and forth quite easily.

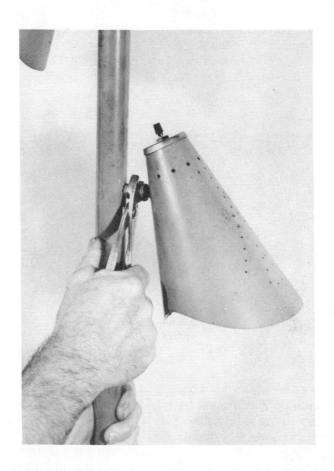

Many low-cost pole lamps have adjustable light-holders with a ball-and-socket joint. You can turn them in several different directions. This turning action eventually loosens the lamps, and they may refuse to stay in the position you want them.

Between this ball and socket joint and the pole, you should find a knurled nut. A pair of pliers will retighten this nut against the ball. The swivel won't be so loose, then. Be careful and don't clamp the pliers too tight or you will scar the nut. Placing a cloth between the pliers and the nut will guard against damage on difficult to turn nuts.

Lamps come under the heading of electrical repairs. They're not dangerous if you don't try foolishly to work with the cord connected to the wall outlet. You should even unplug a lamp before you change a burned-out bulb.

Wear and tear, and gnawing animals, can put a lamp cord in ragged shape. The most wear occurs at the plug, right where the cord goes into it. Next worse wear occurs where the cord enters the lamp housing. Both places should be examined every few months—and oftener as the lamp ages—to spot bare wires before they cause a shock or blow a fuse or circuit breaker.

These pages show how to replace a lamp cord. If you're alert, you'll also see how the socket and switch comes apart for replacement, since the cord photographed here is new all the way from socket to plug. (And that's new too, so you'll also see how to put on a new plug. You may have to cut one off of a frayed cord or replace a broken plug.)

Take off the shade. Then take apart the lamp socket (be sure the old cord isn't plugged in). You may need a small screwdriver to pry the two socket sections apart. Remove the old cord ends from the terminal screws. Cut the cord end clean, but don't pull it out of the lamp yet; it can be helpful in fishing the new cord through.

Buy AWG-18 double lamp cord (POSJ, it's called; and sometimes "zip-cord"). Buy plenty. A 9-foot cord gives you much more freedom of lamp placement than the usual 6-footer. So buy 12 feet to work with. You can cut it shorter if you want to, before you put the plug on.

Fish it through the lamp, from whichever direction comes easiest. You can tape the new cord to the old, but tape it snug so they don't hang up in the cord holes.

Thread the end up through the socket center. Leave about 6 inches of cord sticking out the top. Now split the two wires apart.

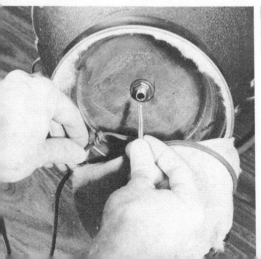

Trim about an inch of insulation off each wire, exposing the stranded conductors. Twist the strands tight in each wire, so no loose strands stick out to cause a short circuit later. If you have soldering equipment, "tin" the strands; that holds them together solidly.

Wrap the conductor of each wire around its respective terminal screw. A clockwise wrap holds best when you tighten the screws. Make the wrap as near to the insulation on each wire as you can; just don't get the insulation under the terminal screws. Snip off the leftover bare wire that protrudes from under the tightened screws.

Pull or feed the wire down into the lamp and reassemble the socket. If you had to take apart the bell that holds the shade, be sure you don't omit that in your reassembly. Pull the cord snug from the bottom. Then, if the other end of the new cord is uneven, trim it.

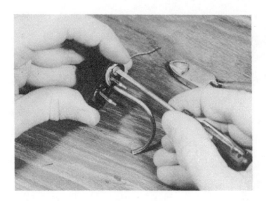

Putting a plug on the free end of the new cord isn't difficult. (This is the same procedure you would follow if you had to cut off a broken plug or cut a frayed cord.)

Thread the cord through the plug. Tie a strain-relief knot about 2 inches from the end. Pull it back down into the plug. Separate the two free wires. Trim off enough insulation to let the stranded conductors reach the terminal screws, but leave enough so the insulation reaches right up next to the screws.

Twist the strands tight. Tin them if you have soldering equipment. Wrap the bare part of each wire around its respective screw. Tighten. Then snip off the excess, close to the screws. That completes the operation, except for putting a cover over the plug prongs—if there is a cover.

Got a fireplace? Here's a fuel-saving hint. During cold weather, keep the fireplace damper closed unless you're using the fireplace. A lot of the warm air in your room will be siphoned up the chimney if the damper is left open. This cools the house and raises your fuel bill.

The damper usually operates by a hand lever. When the damper is closed, the lever is in its downmost position. In warm weather, keep the damper open to improve air circulation in the room—if it is not air conditioned.

If you worry about an occasional insect from outside, hang an insecticide container from the damper handle. One excellent type can be bought at automobile service stations.

And now—to the bedroom. Maybe you've had a bed you were afraid to lie down on for fear it would fold up on you or collapse in a heap. This happens with older beds—and some newer ones—when the ends of the rails, or the fittings that hold the rails in place, become worn or sprung. Here's a good temporary repair. It will last until the budget permits you to buy a new bed.

Take a piece of heavy cardboard. Cut it to the shape shown, a rectangle about 2 by 6 inches. Cut a slot in it.

Slide the slotted cardboard over the end of the hook on the siderail. Replace the rail in its slot in the bedpost. Push down firmly. The cardboard acts as a shim for the worn end of the rail. It tightens the rail against the bedpost and makes the bed more rigid. The shim could be made of wood, metal, or any material that fills up the space.

If that bed is wobbly enough, the siderails may easily spread apart so the slats and springs fall out. This can be traumatic if it happens as you turn over in your sleep. You may decide to spend the remainder of the night sleeping on the floor. But the next morning, fix it.

Remove mattress and springs. Take one of the slats and drill a hole in each end.

Place the drilled slat near the center of the railings and fasten it down with two 1½-inch wood screws. Space the other two slats an equal distance from this center one—one slat toward the foot of the bed and the other toward the head. Have them far enough apart to provide solid support for the springs. Put the springs and mattress back on, remake the bed, and you're ready for some restful, uninterrupted sleep.

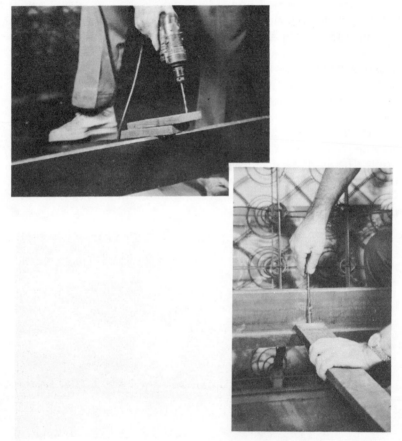

Look at that same old bed. Does it just sit there like a rock during every struggle to clean under and around it? Or maybe cleaning gets put off in that room because it's such a difficult job. The bed may even have had casters at one time, but over the years they have worn out, or got broken or lost. Virtually all beds, whether of wood or metal, have the holes in the legs for casters, with metal liners already inside them.

Modern casters are of a type that look more like a ball than like a whee!. These roll more freely over any surface, bare floor or rug. They cost slightly more than the wheel kind, but are worth the difference. Ask at any hardware store. New metal liners come with them, in case the old liners are missing or don't exactly fit. Just slip the new casters in place.

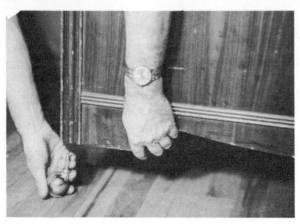

What about the baby bed? Is it swaying back and forth in danger of collapse? Do you feel you'd better buy a new one before it falls and Junior gets hurt?

Before you consign the old bed to the junk heap, look it over to see if anything is actually broken. If it is structurally sound, there's a remedy for the rickety condition.

If you remember when you bought the bed, it was probably unassembled. Just go over the bed now and look for all the screws, bolts, and nuts you fastened it together with. Tighten them all with a screwdriver and pliers. Replace those that are missing or damaged. Chances are the old crib will still serve Junior's needs quite adequately.

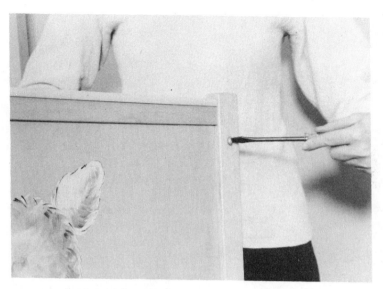

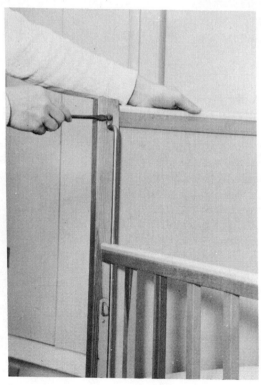

Almost everyone has at least one old drawer that won't open or close easily. First, struggle with it until you get it out. In this process, the drawer is probably already coming apart. Your tugging may worsen its condition, but that can't be helped at this point. It has to be taken out completely before you can be sure what has gone wrong, and so you can work on it.

Once you get the drawer free, look it over carefully. Often you can spot the scrapes that tell you where it was binding. That leads to what was causing it to bind. Before you fix that, though, you'd best get the drawer back together. Suppose the bottom of the drawer has worked loose and has slid part-way out.

Turn the drawer up on its front edge and hammer the bottom gently back into position. There may be nails that have worked loose. They may have been catching in the drawer guides. If so, they are likely bent. Pull them out completely, as it is almost impossible to drive a bent nail back into place. Straighten them first, and then put them back.

Add a few more nails—not so many the wood splits—to make the drawer more rigid. Use three-penny (3d) nails. It's a good idea to use cement-coated types. The friction of driving them into the wood makes the cement soft or tacky and the nails then (when the cement dries) hold much better.

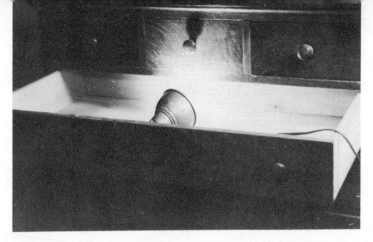

Try the drawer to see if it will go in smoothly. If it still sticks, there is more to do.

The inside and bottom of a drawer seldom have any finish or sealer. These unsealed surfaces absorb moisture in damp or humid weather and cause the wood to swell. The effect can last for days after the humidity drops back to normal.

Put a small lamp, one with a 40- or 60-watt bulb, in the drawer. Let it dry the wood out for several hours. If you don't have a lamp small enough to fit inside, place the drawer near a heat register or electric heater. Don't set it too close. If you use the lamp, don't let the bulb actually touch the wood.

When the drawer is thoroughly dry, you can prevent future trouble. Coat the inside and bottom of the drawer with either white shellac or varnish. This seals the wood and keeps future moisture out.

These materials can be obtained at any paint store or lumber yard. Be sure to specify white shellac. Another kind, called orange shellac, stains what's in the drawer, and wouldn't be suitable for this use.

Let the shellac dry completely. A couple of days wouldn't hurt. Then coat the drawer runners and guides with paraffin. This is the same paraffin wax that is used in the kitchen to preserve jelly and jam. You can buy it at most grocery stores. If you don't happen to have paraffin, you could use the remains of a candle; it's made of paraffin wax too.

If there are still tight places, it's time to put a wood rasp or small smoothing plane to work. Remove a little wood from the bottom edges of the drawer. Avoid taking off very much.

Use care with either of these tools. If you use the rasp, hold it flat to the surface. Grip it with both hands, one at either end. The object is to keep the tool flat so it won't gouge or cup out. The plane is a little easier to use, but you must always go with the grain of the wood. (That's best with the rasp too.) Lift the tool after each one-way stroke, rather than "sawing" back and forth.

Consider the door that will not close and just bangs against the door jamb. This almost certainly means the screws that hold the hinges have worked loose. To fix: Open the door. Wedge a book or a block of wood under the bottom to hold the door in a correct position. Tighten the screws with a screwdriver.

Maybe the screw won't tighten. Back it out completely. Then drive a matchstick or other piece of wood into the empty hole. Now insert the screw and it should tighten okay. It might take two or three matchsticks or splinters to "line" the worn hole. You could perhaps use a larger, slightly longer screw in hopes of biting into new wood deeper in the door frame. Beware, though, of splitting the frame. (A longer screw may not help if it is the door side of the hinge that needs tightening. Some doors are hollow.)

The door may still be sticky. Find the places it drags or fits tight. Slide a piece of paper between the closed door and the frame. Wherever the paper stops sliding, that's where the door is catching. Possibly there are several places. Mark each spot with a strip of masking tape.

There's another way to mark the sticking door. Rub colored carpenter's chalk on the surface of the door frame. Push the door shut. The chalk will rub off at the places that are tight. Open the door and you can see the markings on the door edges.

To cure the tightness, you may have to take some wood off the door itself. The chalk marks or tape are a guide to where the work must be done. Don't try this repair with the door still hanging on its hinges.

Remove the door by lifting the pins out of the hinges. They might be tight. To remove them easily, place the bit of a screwdriver against the head of the pin. Tap the end of the handle with a hammer until the pin loosens. Lift the pin out.

Remove the bottom pin first, then the top one. Should you take out the top pin first, the door might topple over while you are removing the bottom one.

Place the door on edge. With a small smoothing plane, shave off lightly where the tight places are indicated. Do not take off much wood. Replace the door. If it is still tight, repeat the whole marking-and-shaving process. This may seem like a lot of work. But it's better to shave off a small amount at a time than to take off too much and leave a large crack.

Do you have a sliding closet or washroom door that looks like this, sagging and showing a wide crack when closed? The hangers need adjusting. This maladjustment can be caused by the door being opened or closed too forcibly. Or, some object on the floor of the closet may get wedged under the door accidentally. Either one causes the hanger screws to loosen.

These hangers are adjusted from inside the closet. The hanger is a metal plate. Two screws fit in perpendicular slots in the hanger. The slots permit the door to be set higher or lower. Loosen the hanger screws and push the door closed, tight against the door frame. Hold the door in that position and re-tighten the screws. The frame squares up the door.

This could leave the door hanging too low. Too much pressure against the bottom tracks or the floor may make it tough to slide. Put two equal-thickness books under the bottom of the door to hold it up while you adjust. Square the door against the jamb as before and tighten the adjustment screws.

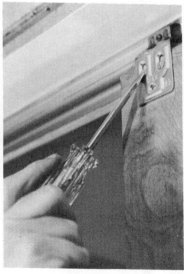

Here's a quickie hint to wrap up this chapter. Don't put up with squeaky hinges. They're too easy to fix. Too, if they're left alone, the squeak becomes a strain and may eventually work the hinge loose.

Door hinges should be lubricated with powdered graphite. Your hardware store has little squeeze tubes of it. To do the lubrication properly, the hinge pins should be lifted slightly. Raise them just enough that you can work graphite onto the pin and down into the hinge.

Chapter 8

Walls, Halls, and Creaky Stairs

Nowhere in the house escapes the attention of an alert and thorough home repair expert. Nor is there any room or alcove that doesn't at some time or other need that attention. Walls and ceilings in every room; stairways to the basement, second floor, or attic; windows; floors; everything sooner or later needs maintenance or repair.

This final chapter illustrates and explains some of the skills you must apply to this all-over-the-house maintenance. Obviously, the time to make most repairs is before they grow so large they need a contractor. You can cut house repair and maintenance costs to less than half if you develop the habit of spotting and correcting "little things" that go wrong. It takes time—yes. You have to weigh whether your spare time is worth the dollars saved in repair bills. For most people, it is . . . and then some.

Many a floor squeaks when you walk on it. But it needn't. Go to the basement or crawl space under the floor and try to locate the squeaky spot. Have someone bounce on the squeaky area till you find one or two squeaky boards. You will likely discover that the floor joists have sagged, leaving certain floor boards unsupported.

If only two or three floor boards are involved, take a wood shingle and split it into 2-inch strips. Drive one or more of these strips between the joist and the floor. This fills the space and should stop the squeaking. It won't stop the floor from sagging further, though (see facing page).

Creaky stairsteps can be repaired the same way if you can reach them from underneath. Insert small shims or wood wedges between the steps and their supports. If the stairway is enclosed, you can still drive a few nails down through the steps into the supports. Use finishing nails—the ones without broad heads. Countersink the heads below the surface with a nail punch. (While you're at it, reset other nails in every step so none protrudes.) Then fill the depressions with plastic wood. Paint them over.

In an old house, supporting beams often sag and cause the floor to become uneven. To remedy this situation, you will need a floor jack, available from a lumber yard. This jack has two pieces of pipe or tubing, a screw assembly, and two steel plates—one to go under the bottom end and another for the top. The bottom pipe is larger in diameter than the top one, and both have holes in them to let you adjust length.

Slide the smaller pipe into the larger. Put the bottom plate on the floor and the large pipe on it. Place the screw assembly on top. Raise or extend the pipes to almost the desired height from basement floor to the support beam. Insert a steel pin, which is provided, through the alignment holes of both pipes. Tighten up the screw assembly until the top of the jack is almost touching the beam. Place the smaller steel plate on top and hold it steady with one hand. Turn the screw assembly more, until the plate contacts the beam.

Make sure the jack is plumb, or straight up and down (see page 31). Tighten it solid. Let it set for a day or two. Then tighten it up a little more. If you try to raise the beam too much at a time you might crack it. Continue in the same manner and over a period of days or weeks you can raise the beam enough to level the floor. Use more jacks if you need to.

OUCH! You shouldn't have leaned that storm window where the wind would catch it. Lay it flat while you take down the rest of them. But of course it's too late to tell you that; you know already. What you need now is guidance for replacing those broken panes. So . . .

First remove all the broken pieces of glass still remaining in the window frame. You'd do better to wear gloves. Might prevent getting a sliver in your finger or slicing a hand accidentally.

Remove all the old putty or glazing compound with a putty knife. Scrape the wood absolutely clean and bare. If it takes a scrub brush, soap, and water, use them. Coarse steel wool or a wire brush can speed this part of the task.

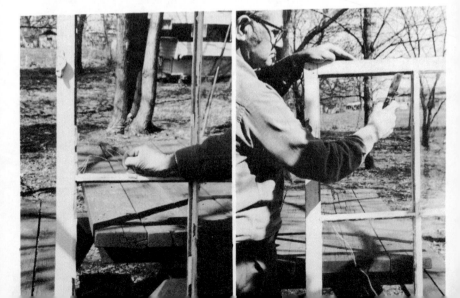

With a folding ruler or yardstick, measure the *inside* dimensions of each empty square in the frame. Measure both directions. Then subtract ⅛ inch from each measurement. This size lets the pane of glass fit into the frame easily. Write the final pane size down, so you don't forget. Measure *all* the empty squares; they might not all be the same.

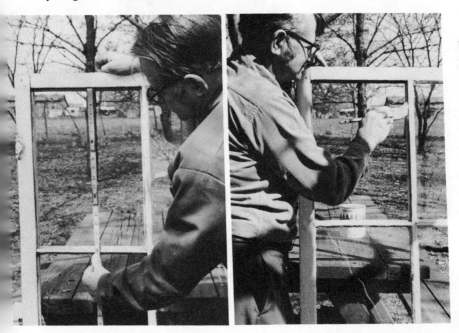

Apply a coat of paint around the groove where you removed the putty. Putty has an oil base. If the groove is not painted, the dry wood will absorb the oil and cause the putty to dry out much sooner. The putty would soon break away, and you'd have the job to do over next year. Let the paint dry completely.

Give them the dimensions of the glass you need, and your lumber yard will cut the panes for you. Buy a can of putty and a small box of glazier's points. Ask for the new type of glazier's points. They have a flat side and a groove across the top. They are much easier to use than the old three-cornered kind.

Place the pane of glass in the frame. Insert a few glazier's points. They hold the glass in place while it is being puttied, and add firmness to the whole job.

Put the flat side of each glazier's point next to the glass. Place either a screwdriver or a putty knife in the groove, and with a little wiggling movement push the point into the wood frame as far as it will go. Be sure it is snug against the glass.

With the putty knife, apply putty all the way around the frame. The putty should be applied as evenly as possible and smoothed out so there are no high or low places. Give the putty a few days to dry. Then paint it to protect it from the weather.

DO NOT try to replace a broken glass in an aluminum storm door or window. Remove the whole frame and take it to a lumber yard or hardware store and have them replace the glass. New government regulations stipulate the kind of replacement (shatterproof plastic).

The clamps that hold the frames in these windows or doors are usually fastened by screws. Loosen them and turn the clamps to one side. You can then lift the frame out.

Anyone who owns or is responsible for the upkeep of a home must spend some time on plaster maintenance. By fixing cracks that appear in plaster walls before they grow, you can save yourself a big-size repair job later on. Left alone, the crack may "meet" another one and a whole section of wall might fall out. This is very common with ceilings.

To fix a crack in the plaster, start by spreading a drop cloth or an old sheet on the floor. That's because you are going to generate some dust.

Then "groove" or clean out the crack. You can buy a tool for this purpose. Or, you can use a three-sided file that has been ground down to a sharp point at the end. Following the crack, groove a channel about ¼-inch deep.

Dip a sponge in water and thoroughly dampen the groove and the surrounding wall area. This will prevent your patching plaster from drying too fast. If it dries too soon, the plaster gets crumbly and falls to pieces before it sets "into" the surrounding plaster.

Buy some patching plaster at any lumber yard. It comes in a small package already mixed, except that you add water.

Adding the water a little at a time, mix only a small amount of the plaster paste. Make sure it is blended to smoothness, with no lumps.

Apply the plaster to the groove with a putty knife. Don't worry if some of the material gets on the wall to either side of the groove. This will easily be removed later. Let the job stand till the putty is entirely dry.

Next, when you're sure the patching is dry, use fine sandpaper to smooth the surface. Now you can see that, although the groove is pretty well filled, it is not yet flush with the surrounding wall surface. Apply another coat of plaster. Let that dry as before. Then repeat the sanding. This time, sand off any excess plaster on the wall near the groove.

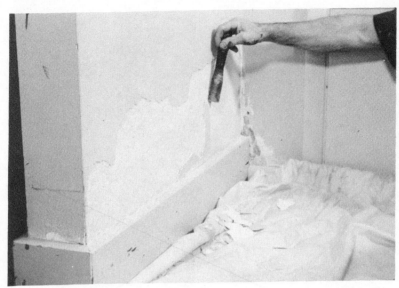

A large area of loose plaster takes relatively the same process, with a few minor differences. You remove all loose plaster with a putty knife. Then you dampen thoroughly the wall area where you have removed the loose plaster, and the adjacent area (to prevent too-fast drying).

Mix the patch plaster to a paste, as you did for repairing a crack. This time, though, since you are working a much larger area, you will need to beg, borrow, or buy a plasterer's trowel. This is a large, flat smoothing tool. This trowel really does two jobs. You use it first of all to apply the plaster to the wall area. Then you use it to smooth the new plaster, making it flush with the surface of the undamaged wall. Hence, you will not need to apply that second coat of plaster.

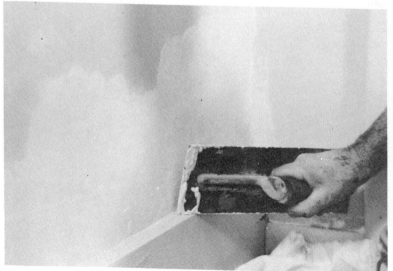

Let the plaster dry thoroughly. This may take overnight, for such a large area. Then use fine sandpaper to smooth the whole patched area. "Feather" it to blend smoothly onto the surrounding wall.

The final part of plastering involves removing all the loose dust. Use the vacuum cleaner and the brush attachment. One final swipe with a slightly damp sponge can remove the last traces of plaster dust.

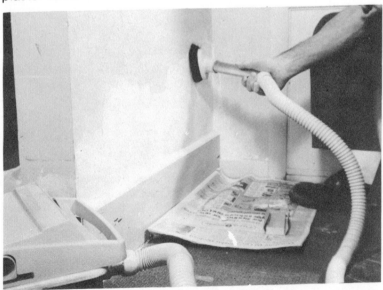

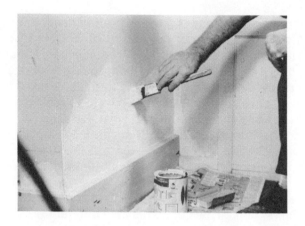

Then you paint. Brush on a prime or first coat of flat paint. Use white or any light color. (Flat paint is a type that dries without any gloss.) After this prime coat is completely dry, apply a coat of either gloss or semigloss paint or enamel to match the paint already on the wall.

A final note: If you have a rough-plastered (textured) area to be repaired, you would proceed almost the same as for smooth plaster. But there are two more steps. After the patch has been applied, notice when the plaster is almost dry but still feels soft to the touch. Then take a dry sponge and rough up the patch. Try to make it look as much like the surrounding wall as possible.

Painting inside a house is a whole craft in itself. Yet the conscientious home-repair buff does a lot of it. Doing your own painting is a great moneysaver. Here are some hints about paints and painting. The proprietor of any paint specialty store can give you a world of additional advice. Don't hesitate to ask. If the help isn't offered cheerfully, go somewhere else to buy.

Make a list before you go. Know what surfaces you want to cover and their dimensions. You'll need mixing buckets, paint pans, brushes, rollers, sandpaper, edgers, and so on. Don't waste effort and money trying to "get by" with junky equipment from some long-ago painting job; buy new.

Be sure you buy the right size and kind of applicators: brushes and/or rollers. Some types of paints take different brushes than others. Get the better grade of brush, with soft, pliant bristles.

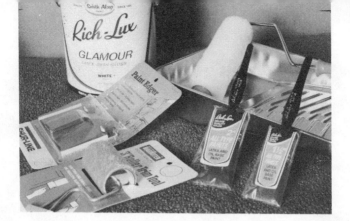

One rule: don't mix types of paint on your walls and ceilings. For example, don't apply paint over varnish, or latex paint over enamel. If you want to change, find out how to prepare the old surface for the new type of finish. You may have to do a lot of "wet-sanding" and perhaps remove the old finish altogether.

Buy whatever kind of paint suits your taste, but stay within the confines of what's best for your surfaces. Bathrooms and kitchens, for example, take flat paints—old-fashioned oil-base, or the newer, easy-to-apply latex semigloss for a very scrubbable surface. A high-gloss latex may suit you better, and can also be washed down easily. For walls of other rooms, latex bases dry quickly and do their own priming and sealing. It may take two coats over some types of old paint.

If you choose varnishes for floors or woodwork, you'll need a sealer first. That reduces how much varnish you use and evens out the appearance of the grain. Pick the new nitrogen-type varnish; it far outclasses the old resin type. The gloss variety gives a clear amber cast to light woods. A dull varnish is best for floors and antiques. Satin varnish lets you work up a hand-rubbed finish on fine furniture or woodwork.

An errand to the attic on a hot summer day probably would sell you on an attic-cooling fan. That trapped heat raises the temperature of the whole house. Lacking a fan, the attic should have windows or louvers (the latter screened) in the gabled ends. You can add an attic exhaust fan. Go to an electrical supply store and select a 24-inch attic fan. You can buy the fan complete with shutters.

Install the fan in one gable end of the attic, between the studs, and as near the center of the gable as is practical. The shutter goes on the outside and the fan on the inside.

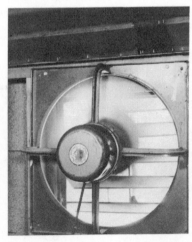

To install, measure the shutter. Inside the attic, mark off an outline with dimensions slightly smaller than the shutter. Work from the inside so you don't hit studs with your sawing. With brace and bit or electric drill, bore a hole through at each of the four corners of your outline. Use a "keyhole" saw to saw out the opening.

Attach the shutter on the outside with its screws. Make sure the shutter operates easily and is not in a bind. Mount the fan so it covers the opening. If all are properly mounted, the shutter stays closed when the fan is not running. When the fan comes on, its breeze opens the shutter automatically.

Pick up power for the fan from the attic wiring. If you are experienced with wiring, you can put the fan on its own individual circuit. If you're not, call an electrician to do the job.

The exhaust fan can be controlled by a manual switch downstairs or by an automatic thermostat. The photo shows a thermostat that starts the fan when attic temperature reaches 85 degrees.

Of course, indoors is not the only place around your house that needs maintenance and repairs. The outdoors is just as important. Whereas the inside gets wear and tear from being lived in, the outside takes abuse from the weather. The home repair expert who really does the whole job spends almost as much time and attention on the outside.

To help with that, there is a companion book to this one. It is *Forest H. Belt's Easi-Guide to Outdoor Home Repairs.* It shows you, by photographs and explanations just as this book does, how to make some of the common and important repairs to the outside of your house. It also includes, as does this volume, directions for saving even more money through preventive maintenance. If you're interested in total home care, you'll want that volume too.